BRIGHT DARKNESS

First Flowstone Press Edition • February 2017
ISBN-13 978-1-945824-06-7

BRIGHT DARKNESS

For Carolyne Wright
Crescent City, CA
9/21/18   K.

POEMS BY
KEN LETKO

LINT

ALL THIS TANGLING

BRIGHT DARKNESS

COMPLETE FRAGMENTS

FORGOTTEN INVENTORS

THE HORIZON IS SO FAR

SHELTER FOR THOSE WHO NEED IT

EVEN BREATHING

BRIGHT DARKNESS

You can only go half way into the deepest forest;
then you are coming out the other side.

Chinese Proverb

LINT

A BRIEF HISTORY OF MOISTURE

snow is purity alive
each grown crystal
the youngest child

snow has been mist
in the redwoods
has been the surf

has ridden a wave
in every ocean
surrounded Elba

before Napoleon
learned to swim
snow has been rain

washing the pupa
of a moth hanging on
through a hurricane

in Haiti every drop
of water is older than all
humans and trout gills

love coldness
in Wisconsin
poplar trees explode

at forty below zero
where Fahrenheit
and Celsius collide

conspiring with crystals
to turn a tree's blood
into unique clear shapes

every puddle on Earth
has climbed a mountain
has been a mirror

has drifted
without a map
as a cloud

LIQUID FIBER AFTER THE FUNERAL

On the kitchen stove the tea
kettle is an opera singer.

Out the window the moon
is a blood-red aria piercing

the ocean, but prayer is one
thing that is always possible.

My prayer and yours are not
the same. Yet we touch.

The ocean is a self-tuning
metronome, and nothing

rides the surf like foam.
Sometimes the sea gulls

know how to say nothing.
Sometimes, they raft up

like the liquid fiber
of a human being

drinking tea while
crying to the horizon.

POCKETS

fog needs a place
to spend the night

flint knife
empty hands

obsidian travels
to the ritual

in a pouch
a kangaroo brings

the kids along
a meteor impacts

the desert, a rocket
just glad to see ya

clothes, keys,
Swiss Army knife,

identification,
lint, payday

mints, money,
matches, maps

employment for
button-down flaps

a small group
of dissidents

a bank shot
in the corner

PEANUTS

the seventh inning
stretch Fenway Park
always cheaper than

cashews and pistachios
peanuts you never look
at yourself in the mirror

because you are
a subterranean legume
that creates tick tack toe

with a fork in a bakery
right brain left brain
you also call out

to onion and garlic
you kiss Halloween
orange and black

sometimes you hang out
with sea salt and beer
and allow radial tires

to plagiarize your imprint
your skin never blushes
but sometimes crumbles

on the dance floor
your red papery film
sticks between teeth

yet a thumb knows
how much stress
you can handle

because of your
symmetrical
split personality

CHANCING DARES
After Picasso's Three Musicians

"Hey," said the shadow
of the table leg. "Can you
play one I know well

enough to dance to?"
"Surely," said the table
top that wanted to be

a dulcimer. Every time the
beard that wanted to become
a scarf tried to join in,

Michelangelo hummed along.
This is the band that filled
the auditorium with dancing

chairs, chancing dares
until the usher stepped
to the center of the stage

saying, "Well, well,
if this were Halloween,
you'd be all set."

Your geometric gumbo
could play a song,
one all can see,

hear with their eyes.
It's a lucky thing
your mustache didn't

get trapped in the clarinet
because your guitar was
two fishbowls of fine

whiskey that spoke
to the shadow
of your dancing foot.

The trapezoid head
memorized it all, even
the dog behind the table.

But the painter, trampled
under the horse hooves
that wanted to be table legs,

only wanted to paint
a picture of the song.

MANNEQUIN WITH TEETH

I had inherited
a large pile of teeth
many baby

teeth a few horse
molars and of course
because my grandmother

was a dentist a very
generous supply of
wisdom teeth

the largest was from
a malformed moose
the smallest from a flea

so when I was hired
to revolutionize the
front window display

of a bridal shop
I knew all
the mannequins

would have to be
constructed from
my collection

my greatest expense
was, of course, for
Super Glue! I used

614 tubes on the
flower girl alone

SURVIVING THE HOUSE FIRE

I wish the pinging in my heart
were only the raindrops
missing you. But the house fire

disfigured even the way
you breathe. So I
don't know where to look

for oxygen or a wine opener.
I lost my Underwood
in the ashes and bulldozer

tracks. I want my lullaby
to reach you,
but it has no arms.

I hope this twisting
of my pencil sings
in a spectrum of light

you can hear. Should I
keep remembering how
to touch you in the place

you invite no other?
Or should I keep hoping
these raindrops will become

snowflakes that have to melt
before they can become a river?
If I could ache more than this

I surely would because my nostrils
have not hovered over your scalp
for so long. The mist

in the redwoods is the largest
happiness we can pass
through but never own.

TSUNAMI

March 27, 2005,
Crescent City, CA,
remembering 1964

on a night like tonight,
and what night is not tonight?
the coals of the fire mellow

down so I can see
how my ancestors
loved their children

I can hear small waves
whimper as they lap
the tide line. The ocean

constantly reshapes
its fingerprint so
it will never be jailed

even though survivors
know who killed
the shoemaker

know who knocked
down the power line
igniting the oil tanks

now ablaze alongside
people who realize
the tsunami

was the accomplice
taking orders
from the fault line

and the waves
that follow

BOBCAT

Nowhere becomes now here
when given the right space,
a bobcat on an evening
prowl or napping comfortably

for the afternoon on a stone
ledge. She has a puckered
grin and tufted ears. Her
wimple marks her reclusive

order, yet in the moonlight
she shows her nameless
twin girls who own peaks
and gullies. Her back,

a spotted reddish brown,
arches a bit as she pounces
on a quail. She loves fresh
flesh but swallows some

feather and bone. Then she
saunters off, knowing
when to purr, when to crouch,
when to expand her range.

For the view, she climbs a live
oak. Her dewclaw, a curved
wire, staples her to a limb,
to her primal churnings.

SALTINES

you have sixteen bullet
holes carefully placed
in your square edition

you fraternize with pickles,
cheese, peanut butter,
chicken noodle soup

your paste sticks
to my teeth and employs
my tongue your oyster

miniatures float like life
rafts in chili saltines you
are my date the night

before payday your pinking
shear lace is the perimeter I
love but my crush on you

helps me fry cod while
attracting ants, mice,
and roaches

PRAYING FOR STRANGERS

The artist buys
a painting.
A coin

in the slot,
every woodpile
is a prayer

for winter.
The chef orders
carryout.

The shriek
of a peacock
is a woman

crying.
A bruised
phantom,

the sprinter
walks home, and
the mechanic

buys a new car.

DIRT

my name
Sunday morning

little secret swept
under the carpet

vacuum cleaner bag
your beautiful bulge

dust bunny, spider
web, coffee spill

Wimbledon
Mesopotamia

mother of all
fingernails dig

in the garden

SKUNK ETHICS

I'm supposed to stink
dig up and eat grubs
paw through garbage

bite marauders who
threaten my babies
transmit rabies

I waddle slowly
even though I
pioneered racing

stripes and I die
on the pavement
more often

than the heroes
of Indy and Daytona
crows ravens and vultures

love me mostly in my
morbid middle of the
road posture

I deserve winters off

POTATO

you've grown up
with beets, radishes,
onions, and carrots

matured into hash
browns, home fries,
baked, scalloped,

whipped your school
buddies called you spud
hot French fries

you witness so many
first French kisses
in the back booth

of the Sweet Shop
on Saturday
afternoons

you are too hot
to handle but no
one goes hungry

when you're passed
around you melt
butter and cheese

potato your whiteness
is so full of darkness
you pull the hearse

through the tunnel
to the supper table
one place left empty

boiled, rounded russet
with mayonnaise, mustard,
onion, a little fresh dill

you fill out Bupka's
Sunday dress so
perfectly, potato

CARROT

you are the splash
of color in coleslaw
the wheels in beef

stew carrot you
spend your life
in darkness

hoping you have
the stamina
to winter over

in well-drained soil
your orange bottom
includes a discussion

of hair like your pale
look alike the parsnip
you wonder whether

a gopher will come along
yet you travel well
riding in a backpack

you return to the darkness
of your childhood
the day hikes the picnics

carrot sticks you're
a dieter's best friend
and you attend many

art openings
and poetry readings
the line of people

waiting to sign
a petition denouncing
you is short

and nonviolent

DISHES

The dishes are god.
Kids have to clean their plates,
or there's hell to pay.
Dad stays up after the party
until the last one is put away.
When relatives arrive unannounced,
the dishes say who's lazy.
Dishes mate for life,
but chips and breakage can
destroy the marriage.

LINT

the lint ball in the laundry
room grows because I can't
throw anything away

most loads have been dark
some gray none pure white
most heavy a few light

the big brown blob
is from the blanket
I keep behind my pickup

seat you borrowed it
to catch a gull
with a broken wing

Lucy the Golden Lab
makes her furry entrance
to let us know

that everything
cast away
can cling together

ALL THIS TANGLING

CREATING SAND

now on the other side
of its journey cooled
and resting a meteorite

the size of a bowling ball
rolls with the ocean waves
Atlantic bluefish swim

and day breaks while a phoebe
calls from shore together
sunlight and a flying

cormorant create a moving
shadow that changes shape
rapidly conforming to

the high tide waves turn
and recede from the coast
like a bricklayer stepping

away from the wall
at lunch break igneous
stones rock with ocean

waves and fraternize
with the meteorite
together they are

parents of sand

FEWER WORDS

silence is docile
but the highest
form of communication

some people climb
mountains in search
of it even in China

a walnut tree knows
it should be among
the first to lose

its leaves the closer
together two people get
the fewer words they need

MOVING ON

remove the rubber band
from the map
planes need extra

power for takeoff
a row of trees
slows the wind

the Chinese
invented money
to make barter

easier a cicada
poses long
the artist

creates lines like
small skyrockets
at night lovers

who have grown
tired of each
other find ways

to wander off

ENOUGH

dirty snow
loiters along

the interstate
a twisted brown

bag is paralyzed
wrapping a bottle

that waits to be
buried when

it storms
a hitchhiker

remembers broken
mirrors still

reflect and foam
survives a waterfall

in an apartment
in Cleveland a white

flower is enough
for a shamrock

ADAPTATION

a jogger along
the highway listens
to recorded
bird songs

behind a tavern
a blue jay builds
a nest from plastic
six-pack holders

late in the afternoon
tonight's band sets up
the guitar player has
callused fingertips

on the radio a Native
American sings a Hank
Williams song the news
caster says pandas

reproduce in captivity
across the highway
patrolling a cemetery
the tip of a pine tree

is a great horned owl

STRANGER

follow your heart
bulges in a city

light tremolos
from traffic

the visitor walks
past a wine bottle

and looks back
in the window

a dog food display
is a water fountain

when he arrives
at the hotel

closing the blinds
stirs glowing embers

the shower sounds
like a waterfall

and the stranger
knows how far

his ancestors
have taken him

AROUND THE CORNER

in another
neighborhood
where all night

the stars are only
stars and seldom
even considered

the police department
is called when all else
fails or it's too late

the victim tripped over
crack on the sidewalk
a man with a cell phone

is really connected
to a twelve-year-old
boy with a shotgun

lookout patrolling hell
this ain't no two bit
scam this is what flashes

past a citizen whether
or not he or she votes
for president or trash

collector who doesn't
mention the cash or body
in this week's haul

THE STREET AT 9:00 A.M.

checks cashed checks
cashed checks cashed
no id required checks

cashed here twenty-
four hours a day no
waiting in the street

a woman with a paper
cup and a cardboard
sign says I'll work

for food a white
cat laps at a puddle
of antifreeze dripped

from the radiator
of a parked car
checks cashed here

never closed checks
cashed checks cashed
beer and wine at state

minimum a small girl
drags one winter mitten
a string through her

coat sleeve the other
end in her mouth she
chews the wet thumb

in her right hand
Mamma's a rock
monster stomping

toward a black
leather jacket
under a backwards

Oakland Raiders
duck bill hat
that rolls on

a skateboard checks
cashed checks cashed
in neon checks cashed

LIGHTING THE STOVE

unfold magic with a match
the flame eats darkness

curls of redwood and fir
stripped with a knife

each piece unique life
the flames touch parents

swage the future
glass is liquid stone

a cat with a bald chin naps
meat and water the night

is where all humans live
at least half their lives

home is the controlled
glow and the woodpile

disappears like heat
light and smoke

AS PERSONAL AS SLEEP

a murder of crows
clusters in a tree
near a carcass

of a road kill
that draws heat
to the pavement

like a black roof
where the glint
of a shingle-stone

reflects the silence
of a hair falling
from a sleeper's

head covered by
burning forsythia
yellow but not consumed

since dreams come back
sometimes in rags tired
flags waving or a black

feather falling without
wind spinning a sleeper
may be of any race

because sleep knows
all and grants fortune
to those who rest

HUMANS

skull plates join
all together
the crowd breathes

each lung a dark
balloon close
to a heart

both sides power
the brain and walk
on two legs hold

hands with a child
and reach upward
leaves unfold

in sunlight a river
and the shadow
flow as continents

position themselves
under the stars

ALMOST RAIN

the drought's front
end lingers while
a boat-tailed grackle

lands at a dried
puddle and crouches
in the shade folding

its wings out and down
near the courthouse
the wind snaps a flag

hard but the mayor
doesn't open the door
a house finch finds

moisture in a mulberry
while a mud crack
opens wider the sun

further penetrates
earth and the workers'
fingers won't heal

because they must join
concrete drain pipes
that lead all the way

to the racetrack
which roars going
nowhere in the heat

RAINDROPS

wash the bell
while it rings
in the schoolyard

another year
takes a last lap
around the racetrack

a rainstorm approaches
as the swimming
pool empties

in the past
the schoolyard was
raucous as the bell rang

everyone ran one
last minute before
getting in line

the ten-year-old
had a reason for
being different

like a rainstorm
not always wanted
even in farm country

doors are some-
times locked but
often left open

maybe a neighbor
just stops by
or a sparrow

is a prisoner
behind the afternoon
shower the drops

remembered for those
who have cried
in a schoolyard

COMING BACK FROM A DREAM

an owl hunts the back
yard where rabbits
eat their grayness

and inside the house
the sleeper still reclines
coming back from a dream

to rediscover a world
where the shadow of a stop
sign is a dark cat

but only as strong
as the shadow of a dove
on a stone wall beside

a road where a frozen
flattened glove is dead
on the pavement the hand

of every human being
reaches out to a cloud
that challenges a parade

of moonlight streaming
down to illuminate
the annihilation

of tenderness and salt
resembling heavy
diamond crystals

A SMOKE AFTER THE ACCIDENT

to remove the smoke
from a cigar he sucks

drawing the glance
of the whole barroom

the draperies illustrate
slender sticks burning

faster than plump round
ones he wishes he could

withstand the pressure
a lake trout manages

at three hundred feet
with only fins and tail

lights swerving
the Buick will never

be the same in a junkyard
his insurance policy

seems to be an aqueduct
tilted up but running

down the broken mirror
in the rest room

IN SAN FRANCISCO,
REMEMBERING A
CRATER LAKE SUNSET

a piece of plate glass
separates steaming cappuccino
from a cup of coffee gone

cold and is the barrier
between a tweed that lounges
on mohair and damp denim

on a blanket on concrete
in the shoe store entrance
alcove across the street

the peaks of both buildings
reach for the same evening
sky that knows no hard line

exists between hot and cold
between black and white red
gloaming joins the darkness

that fills the Pacific
and Crater Lake

THE COASTAL TRAIL TURNS
INLAND AND RISES UP

darkness still quiets the ocean
the fire builder rolls out
of a damp sleeping bag sips

pale stars breaks redwood duff
into perfume and kindles a light
calling to the eastern kindred

glow protected from the ocean
by a dune a lagoon lies below
flat shaped by sand eastward

the trail rises up and inland
blackberry lashes a little
used side path a squadron

of meadowlarks catapult the hiker
remembers the ginkgo biloba
was the first to bloom the spring

after the bomb at Hiroshima
remembers a Native American
museum with a musket barrel

cut off and drilled into a flute
remembers when the trail rises
up high enough manzanita

new and old twisted together stands
on a root broad and wide a pelvis

TOGETHER

many muscles move
as a human eye
opens a flock

of sparrows
eating seeds
along a stone wall

scatter when a car door
slams in the Sunday
paper the Soviet Union

dissolves a dandelion
tuft is a spider a dry
oak leaf a sparrow

wars of the world
have been enough
China is two billion

eyes watching sparrows
regroup and land

SANCTUARY

the yellow furnace
of buttercups

vandalizes darkness
in the morning

Indian paintbrushes
climb a ravine

ushering some nymphs
that have become

dragonflies this meadow
is a crematorium

purified by daisies
on one a damselfly

folds its wings and rests
bank swallows catch insects

in flight but not all
bugs perish easily

the fire doesn't tire
only the fuel quits

at night while a few
insects die of old age

the paintbrushes
descend the ravine

CAMP TOGETHER

six hundred miles today
the hatchback is parked
under a box elder small

twigs burn with bright
light while birch coals
juggle campfire flames

on a ridge a coyote jumps
out of its shadow howling
at the deaf moon suddenly

a cloud is a feral horse
that tramples moonbeams
in silence there is all

this tangling in reflected
light which is unable
to travel any other way

COMPLETE FRAGMENTS

UNGLUED

Imagine that today all the glue
in the world let loose. False
teeth drop as fast as wallpaper

peels. Wooden furniture
collapses. In supermarkets
labels and price tags remove

themselves. The butcher's block
becomes kindling. At the post
office and in mailboxes, envelopes

open. The vase you broke as a child
and put back together, without anyone
knowing, is in pieces again. Bumper

stickers litter the highways. Perfect
book bindings release their pages.
The gasket on your refrigerator door

becomes a snake on the kitchen floor.
The bottoms of your shoes fall off.
Model airplanes disintegrate. The man

in the Wonder Glue commercial gets crushed
by the piano. The fletching falls
from an arrow in mid-flight. The patched

tires on your bike go flat. The guitar
under your bed explodes in its case.
America's eyes leave the T.V. screen.

ABSORBING THE BROADCAST

Waves are penetrating
our bodies constantly.

We hardly ever realize
it, but they are always

passing through our
brains and bones. Our

future will be greatly
affected. Waves cannot

be escaped. Our bodies
absorb them as most matter

must. They're ubiquitous,
just waiting for someone

to power up a laptop. So
go ahead because even

if you're not listening
or watching, you are still

absorbing the broadcast.

I WILL NEVER

create oxygen
lick my tongue
or breathe

backwards
I can't
touch

my own nose
with my tongue
I don't want to

dissect myself
count to a
billion or

become a
trapezoid
I can't

prosecute
or tickle
myself

won't survive
without water
or willingly

turn into steam
it's impossible
for me to thrive

on radioactivity
or stay in shape
without skin

WITHOUT LANGUAGE

In a world
without language

what good would
a telephone be?

Radio advertising
would disappear.

Instrumental music
would become more

popular. Television
would have sound

effects but no
dialogue. Roadside

motel signs would be
complete vacancies.

Restaurant menus
would be bland.

Braille would be
out of touch.

The Postal Service
would expire.

This poem would
not exist.

THE ELM

This elm he has
cut down was a victim
of the beetle. For many
summers it provided
shade. For many seasons

it was a sturdy friend
with whom he shared
the long slurred whistles
of cardinal, the movement
that gives shape to

wind. He cut the limbs
into firewood, raked
into a pile the twig
branches. He observed
how the smoke filtered

migrations, how
ashes became soil.

THE WAY TIME PASSES

The thin tight
wall of a balloon
is attacked by air

pressure. There is
resistance but with
time air is always

allowed to seep
through. Can you
picture the idea?

Maybe like roots'
growth filtering
through earth. Maybe

like time passing
through us instead of us
passing through time.

THE MARSH

a shorebird
this morning

my life dips
inner spirit

crumbles
like shale

tonight in
moonlight

cattails
in a swamp

are candles
the marsh

is deep
as sky

WHERE BOULDERS SPLIT

If these windows were
prisms, your vision
would separate. Instead

you see an autumn moon
cooling a sky with geese
moving away like summer.

Beyond sky you see days
as perfect as crystals,
ice on stone, dripping

in sun, freezing by
moon. Geometry forming
in the cool bright darkness

where boulders split.

MOQUAH, WISCONSIN

At the wet end of summer,
I stood on a logging scar
of yellow Cat torn scree
speaking in sobs less
solid than screams.

Now, in this magic winter,
I feel dormant cones under
my tracks become maps
drawing me toward spring
planting furrows more

comfortable than dreams.

THE LONG CALM

May we be like birch
comfortable in rags

or radiant like new
lake ice in sunlight.

May we share the growing
weight of winter. Ice

in coldness becomes
stronger, expands from

its source. Clearly
unique we are the same

waiting for the long calm
of hibernation to be over.

DETOX

for J.W. Rice

when the room
explodes he

breaks like a
game of eight

ball he says
the three is

a geranium
trickling in

the corner
of his life

he wants
to dry out

if only a brain
could be well

drained like a
mountain range

no matter how
rained on

it is
solid

REFRESHMENT

She is thin, bright,
and pretty—a coat
of lacquer brushed on

her fingernails.
She gestures to
him. Come into a

conversation. He says,
yes, I'm a complete
fragment, half a

watermelon after
slicing assembled
on a platter. Cool

refreshment, she says,
on a hot summer day is
something we all need.

VIBRATION

You are hitchhiking.
Inside your ear,

the throb of crickets
tells you the human

race is breathing
together creating

energy. You conceive
a wind making strangers

hold onto each other.
Individual interiors

convert into currents
capable of cruising

molecules and galaxies.
Feel the connection.

Climb into a convertible.
The city begins.

Pulsing inward bound
headlights are one

continuous homogeneous
molecular distribution.

Outward bound are
permanent movement.

ATLANTIC CITY, NEW JERSEY

Along the shore,
anodized aluminum
railings lead me.

Near a new plank
in the boardwalk,
a snapping

turtle shell
decorates
cool sand

on an overcast
day. People talk
as they drift

home. I visit
only the coast
and have no

conversations.
The ocean cannot
hear me breaking.

THE REFRIGERATOR

Every time you
open the door

the light goes
on in a desert.

One last thread
of string cheese

is a praying
mantis blending

into metal shelf
grates. A small

outcropping of
peanut butter is

a mountain climber
clinging to the side

of a jar. One parsnip
is the finger

of a child pointing
to a mirage of milk.

One third of a bottle
of rosé wine wiggles

when you close the door.
The light goes out.

STAYING CLOSE

The ocean permits me to
immerse myself any time
I care to. The moon stays

out all night. Why have I
spent so much of my life
trying to be like an ant,

nine times stronger than
a human. Birds find shelter
when it storms, and weasels

turn white in winter. Deep
inside I know my ancestors
learned to cook food and

keep their eyes clear
of smoke while staying close
to each other and the fire.

THE CYCLE

as rain falls
to the ground
so do blossoms

in the spring
they don't complain
because the cycle

rises when leaves
grow and water
reaches a body or

moves through gills
and around shells
seas form shores

coastlines give
shape to oceans
and water is

shared by all

FORGOTTEN INVENTORS

THE IMPORTANCE OF SLEEP

last night I sat
by my grandmother
in her perfect
broken English

she helped me
understand
the sound of
her back porch

screen door slapping
shut is the call
of every redwing
blackbird

COMING HOME TO SUNDAY

By the time I've slipped
the key into the lock,

she's already sitting
on the chair by the door.

I enter, pick her up,
and lift her above my head.

Laying her right side on the
top of my skull, I gently

shake my head so I massage
her ribs. Then I lower her

belly to my face and love
bite her. She purrs, licks

my left ear, and love bites
my ear lobe. I set her down

on the chair. I am home.

THE LOST PART

the little spring
that puts pressure
on the tiny lever
fell into the grass

the actor's role
written out, muffler
on a highway, her
hysterectomy

bald now, I used to
part on the left
the sign says
"whole chickens

with parts missing,
ten percent off,"
the butcher's
phantom thumb

GYPSY FREEDOM

Gypsies weave halters
from horse hair so horses
can control themselves.

At eighteen Django Reinhardt
put his soul into a guitar.
An enclosed wagon

is a traveling bedroom.
A man and a woman
can love each other

without speaking. A sandbar
shows up for the low tide.
Losing two fingers

doesn't have to end a career.
A bridge helps guitar strings
cross the North Sea,

and the singer remembers
the next verse. Nostrils
are not the only way

to breathe. Horses gulp air
whether they gallop
or drag a stone boat.

SILICA

inside a grain
of sand
is the volcano

outside a grain
of sand
is the ocean

the tribal trail
ascends
from the beach

washed first
then leading
to the caldera

NIGHT SUPERVISION

Axes are like children,
sons and daughters,

who should not be left
out alone overnight.

The darkness seeps in,
loosens the head.

THE POWER OF LIGHT

can turn a white
dog black
a silhouette

on the horizon
sunlight unfolds
every new leaf

pulls a sumac
sprout through
four inches of asphalt

a red light stops a chain
of fast-moving cars
at an intersection

light you spend
all day every day
at the end of the tunnel

nine missing miners
on the windowsill
nine candles

widow's walk
a lantern for
a late boat

the moon
is your proxy
interrogating

the night sky
you can make
mud shine

any student
of the stars
knows the sky

can be any color

RANDOM PATTERN

dune grass thrives
in the thin unstable
sand and the ocean

is the world's largest
collection of tears
this is why so many

people remove their
shoes and socks
when they walk

on the beach but
prefer to leave
their sunglasses on

TRUTH

No opossums live under my living room rug.
The dog barking in the midnight street is a drunkard laughing.
A bucket of water is a great way to spend the afternoon.
At age forty-five I discovered radishes as a favorite snack.
A hubcap shot with a shotgun makes a good colander.
Draft beer is dolphin-free.
A caged bobcat is a dangerous pillow.
Singed hair smells like nothing else.
Old bones in the silverware drawer have divided a marriage.
The old gray mare has ninety feet of intestine.
Dust is brighter than thunder, raindrops louder than stars.
Starfish die quietly.

SWAMP

here the humming
bird builds its nest
from spider webs

here the discarded
paperclip looks
like a trombone

here the pin oak
holds its leaves
all winter

ON THE BEACH
Crescent City, California

Because you are from
the golden horse country
hills of California, this sand

beach is a memory of your first
lover on a cool night away from
home. And I'm from Wisconsin,

so the sea lions tonight sound
like thousand pound marine
coyotes. We lie on a blanket

in the firelight, kisses tasting
like forever. With this redwood
root as our shelter from the ocean

mist, we are both fifty,
so we are a century
on the beach.

FORGOTTEN INVENTORS

the turtle
is the architect
of all helmets

the jaybird
invented
the alarm clock

and a murder
of crows discovered
the first audio

alarm system
earthquakes
planned the first

jigsaw puzzle
sea lions designed
swim fins

a mosquito
piloted the initial
drill bit

bananas
engineered
raincoats

pickerel
pioneered
wetsuits

elephants
modeled
the garden hose

LIMP

a low bean ball in the seventh
curled up on the couch Sunday afternoon
dropped a brick Monday morning
a new pair of pumps after the prom
slid into second in the bottom of the ninth
seventeen wheelbarrows of sand
linguini ready for white sauce
a minor rollover on Highway 8
raw bacon into the pan
a horse named Charlie

GENUFLECTION

Each morning the mountain
climbs out of darkness.
Before blossoming,

the wild iris is a spear,
poking the sky. After a hail
storm bombs an open field,

a butterfly passes by.
The wind doesn't ask
the grasses to genuflect,

but they do because
a pregnant wolf carries
the unborn into the attack.

Caught in a spider web,
a dead blade of grass
sways in the wind,

a safe place
to cross the river.

WATER CHOREOGRAPHS BIRDS

snowflakes don't
strut like ravens
but raindrops do

when they gather
on a windowpane
crowing in silence

juncos rinse their
pleated skirts in
snow-melt puddles

as they stroll
toward the ocean
a pair of doves

can't stop sleet
from passing
between them

INSTINCT

For some, things
come so easily.

The young mother
puts three raspberries
in a paper cup that her
three-year-old daughter
carries from room to room,
laughing.

Then there's the nine-year-old boy
who reaches out his arm
to his younger brother, saying,
"Wait, we can't cross yet."

But not me, I still struggle at 53,
staying up late most nights,
watching the fire, trying to see
where the flame ends
and the smoke begins.

DEAR ANDY WARHOL

in 1968 you were right
everyone wanted fifteen
minutes of celebrity

but in 2011 the search
has begun for fifteen
minutes of anonymity

see you on the
other side

THE HORIZON IS SO FAR

IN THE HOSPITAL PAINT SHOP

The top of my work bench
is a door broken through
by a patient on his way
from the psych wing
into story-colored pages.

The invitation
could have been a girl
pretty as bull thistle
lavender in July
her dress
pockets of lightning
horizon dancing
come on
come on.

It could have been
a piece of red apple skin
stuck between two teeth
irritating the tongue
twisting without results
come on come on
get out get out.

Or was it
a jay bird calling
through that door
are the free flapping
story-colored pages
come on come on.

HER MEMORY

He says it keeps
coming back to
him. Silent chant

that is a
boomerang
he can't

stop himself from
throwing. Dreams
all night slant,

shadows flying.
He tosses quietly
and only wants

her ghost to stop.

INCARCERATION

Outside, gargoyle's teeth
speak with sunlight. Inside,

this county building lilts
every day. Happy people,

forms filled out correctly.
Matters of state, stated so

they matter. But the jail!
He cannot see inside. So he

imagines it to be like sleep,
a refuge to some, a nightmare

to others, always inescapable.

VIETNAM VETERANS MEMORIAL

The wall is a stone
bandage in quiet repose
where 1959 touches 1975.

Buis and Greer close
the perimeter—suture
the wound. Mementos

left by family members
and friends are vigils
all night. Purple hearts

pound, but antiseptic
makes no sound like
the left flank—Anderson,

Barnhart, Bates, Blanksma.
On the right flank Vrankovich,
Whitehill, Williams, and Alba

watch the dark granite
for a shadow of a wing
tip, touching only air.

The jungle is one voice.

INSPIRATION

a tall willow
calls after
a rain

a puddle
reflects
while he

falls in
his brain
and knows

collapsing
would feel
good but—

getting back
up is harder
than weeping

on his feet

GLOAMING

As I walk along the edge
of the abandoned quarry,
I see a dead maple with

leaves still clinging
to it. I approach, hear
silence and lean as I

look out where last summer
we swam. Now in early winter,
thin ice is clear. I walk out

over shallow ripple marks,
sliding on the balls of my
feet. The ice bends a bit

and I try to make my whole
body light. I move west.
When I get out over a drop

off, maybe a hundred feet,
I sidle back to shore. On
the bank, doves peck gravel

and coo. There is no snow
anywhere. I keep walking
into the sun, knowing a ring

glows continuously
as it circles the Earth,
separating night and day.

LIBERATION

She is big.
Her voice
is a piano.

Trout brook
waterfall language
is her beauty.

Mid-air droplets
arc into color,
music to see.

Her rhythms harmonize
height, depth, intensity.
With each breath she

moves every molecule
of the universe.

THE WOMAN WHO WALKS THE BEACH AT DAWN
Crescent City, CA

1. She knows

The Black-crowned night heron
inherits the dawn in a tide pool
where pink starfish devote

themselves to existence. Exiting
the cabin on the cliff above,
she quietly closes the backdoor

not wanting to wake her lover
whose head is crowded
with juniper and pinyon pine,

pygmy forest of Utah. She steps
out from him through a wisp of fog
and down the trail to the beach.

The heron notices the smallest
movement underwater and strikes
with a poking and closing jaw,

but the woman walks past this
because she searches for agates
and smooth stones that ride

quietly in the hand or pocket.
A low tide puts the oyster
catchers and whimbrels to work,

and she knows this too but walks
on for the new day, for the sand.
And she returns to lay smooth

stones in patterns on her lover's
porch where the light of an old
fire arrives with the sun.

2. He dreams

If the ocean can brawl with boulders
and the scapula of a sea lion
can become a hoe before disappearing,

then Tibetan bells can ring as
madrone coals crumble or a few
empty coat hangers bump together.

At the fireplace, nuptial ice cubes
chime the wedding of light and shadow
and charm the dancers, bits of ash

drifting from fire. He knows her
breasts are hot doves, the permanent
dreams that make home, home.

3. The night heron knows

Rest between visits to the tide
is a comfort. Fishing singly
is best and sudden strong wing beats

make an escape from danger
possible. But the nest is best
approached in a glide ended

by a timed holding back of wings
just before the feet make
a solid, gripping connection.

SILENT LANGUAGE

Here they are
in Galapagos,
Ecuador looking

for a constant in
their lives. Tonight
the Big Dipper is

upside down.
In their eyes,
water shimmers

at the arrival
of starlight.
In their minds,

light crosses
a galaxy. In
their travel,

silent language
brightens them.

STAYING AHEAD

The color of sun
leads him through
green reflections
given off by plants.

Other hues are
absorbed, needed
by life that is
rooted in earth.

He decides how to cast
his shadow, as he moves
through woods, staying
ahead of his memory.

SNAIL

Glean
from spiral
snail tracks

how slowly
he has wrapped
himself

no one
can see
how he eats

how he walks
the same
foot he hides

draws him

RAIN

near equinox
they travel

in trees color
moves yellow

wind shouts
twirling orange

laughter when
they reach camp

hillside is
their horizon

campfire shadows
blow into trees

on coals rain
begins hissing

SNOWFALL

They wake
to the first

snowfall of winter.
Predawn morning is

cool bright
illumination.

Crystalline vapor
is riding wind,

spirit of winter
flying, accumulating,

radiating bright
silence. This is

the sound
of all color.

INFATUATION

She is beautiful
to him now. Wet

snow clings to
outstretched limbs.

They bend to embrace.
The storm is nearly over.

THE HORIZON IS SO FAR

the ocean is
flat at dawn

after curving around
the earth all night

they walk on white
sand and remain

rational enough to
keep from falling

in love they want
their hearts

to quiet down
for a while

phosphorous quits
glowing at daybreak

plankton float
and drift on

the horizon
is so far

they would be fools
to stop walking

Shelter For Those
Who Need It

FIRST LIGHT
at Lou Guan Tai, for Lao-tzu

The ginkgo biloba
streams down fans
of maiden hair

mourning the haze
burned off by sun-
light and praising

the mica faces
caught in a stone
held by a root.

This silent echoing
marks a place that
a person can run to

when he isn't
running away
from anything.

ABERDEEN HARBOUR, HONG KONG

When the ocean moves
the sail of a Chinese
junk is a giant sea

shell filled with wind.
On deck people hunker
around a charcoal fire

talking together, tea
in metal cups warming
hands. Ashes tossed

overboard float awhile
before sinking to cover
dynasties of refuse.

On grass mats behind
rattan walls, a family
nestles, trying to dream

a future. Under the ship
fish swim all night, symbols
of what needs to be done

sometimes, forever.

THE RAINY SEASON

Wearing a rain poncho
made from kitchen table
oilcloths, a mule plods
along a muddy road

pulling a load of red
bricks on a two wheeled
cart. The driver sits
on a soggy straw mat

on top the bricks. He
holds an opened but torn
umbrella in one hand. As
the cart turns onto paved

Chang An Road, brownish
clods of wet loess fly
from the wheels while
the mule, cart and driver

find their places
in traffic. Tractors,
buses, wheelbarrows,
bicycles and pedestrians

absorb them. A man selling
a pig cut into quarters
at the roadside has two
umbrellas tied to a tree

limb to keep the meat
from getting wet. A man
in a business suit rushes
somewhere with a pink

and white striped towel
on his head, a sheik
in the rain. Another
man in military green

forges onward; a desk
drawer turned up-side-
down and held overhead
is an awning that keeps

him dry. A plastic bag
snugged over a straw hat
protects a young woman
on a bicycle. With brakes

too wet to stop, she coasts
through an intersection,
a cape made from a gunny
sack trailing behind her.

TONG CHUAN, SHAANXI

Cottonwood fuzz drifts
through the afternoon.

A few garbage bees
pester a white goat

that rummages along
the trail to the river.

Some women squat
on flat rocks, washing

clothes in the brown
water. Upstream, naked

children splash knee
deep as they chase.

And the fathers are
up on the brown patches

between the green plots
of wheat. They follow

oxen and wooden plows
through fields terraced

by generations. Above
a pair of magpies cry.

RAINBOWS

don't live long
but they do live
at least in eyes

urgently searching
the rain for beauty
that struggles

with the churning
clouds schooled
by centuries knowing

there is peace where
so much energy is
riding on the narrow

until the image
is murdered
by the light

which is sure
to follow

ACROBAT

Her props can get aboard
the wrong train or a stage
hand can forget to turn up

the lights or bring down
the curtain. The audience
can refuse to applaud,

ignore the most difficult
trick or even forget
to show up. The coach

sometimes yells when
no one is at fault
or when the performance

is tight as leotards.
But the acrobat must rely
on gravity to pull on her

and her body to pull back.

IN CHINA

animals speak Chinese
dogs say wang wang
ducks say ga ga and
roosters say wuuuuwu
pigs say heng heng
and the fish use a
sign language that is
especially difficult
to understand

OUT THE WINDOW

After clasping socks
and shirts flapping
on a line, clothespins

become birds resting
between songs praising
in silence the grasses

bowing in the breeze.
Saved from breaking
these pliant plants

continue performing,
clinging to earth
creating oxygen so

birds can breathe
and freshen the wind
that dries clothes.

CHINESE FAST FOOD

a pretty girl
with a sugar
cane walking

stick takes
a bite chews
then spits

in the street
other people
eat yams

like ice cream
cones wrapped
in newspaper

steamed bread
is a hot snow
ball consumed

by a passenger
side saddle on
a Flying Pigeon

bicycle made
in China like
many kinds of

fast food

BUILDINGS

Before the storm
prevailing winds

hunch the trees.
Rigid structures

resist and people
lean into their

steps. After a
tornado broken

timber and toppled
bricks lie together.

But people rebuild
cities. Straight

cairns rise for
the fallen, new

shelter for those
who need it.

THE LAND

No matter who uses it
the shovel shines all
day and roots stretch

a little before a tree
is pulled out. Clouds
pamper the mountain

while workers lacerate
a switchback. On a train
in the valley foreigners

contemplate China. People
with tools make a mountain
accommodate travel. And

the rail curves, moving on.
But the land doesn't care.
It is only there, a solid

place where nations meet.

PEOPLE LEARN

Flocks of birds
swarm into virgin
timber roosting
all night to rest
for the journey.

Rivers don't know
where they're going.

Schools of fish enter
the always open mouth
appearing confused as
they mingle and press
against the current.

Rivers don't know
where they're going.

Boulders become rounder
while silt travels on
and water makes cradles
that nurture and hold
civilizations.

Rivers don't know
where they're going.

People learn how to
swim and steer boats.
as they follow rivers,
everyday their hair
grows longer.

XIAN, SHAANXI

Down from the Gobi
a yellow wind brings
dust in spring,

making people
cover their eyes
with their hands.

Mouths shut tight
people angle from
shelter to shelter.

After some rain
a morning fog
soothes the valley.

Sunbeams pull
corn and wheat
taller, acres

at a time
like April
in Ohio.

TRAILS

Like water they find
their ways over gravel

and around rocks. They are
where foot meets mountain.

And where trees offer
shade to travelers

who stop to rest. Trails
lead nations onward and

are left behind by comets
and bandits who disappear

into midnight alibis
winding like canyons.

Trails are what become
roads when people think

there is something
at the end worth seeing.

A trail is something
that a person wants

to find when lost or
when wilderness starts

closing in at twilight.

EVEN BREATHING

EVEN BREATHING

opposing shores
support the river

our night
time breathing
collects in a pillow

even though the ocean
tide reverses the river

our breathing produces
the bright cloud we
become on the other side

beneath the surface
loose rocks continue
their muted rattle

while the river otter
generates crayfish
shell mosaics

on a sandbar entrance
to the cave of in and out

the river authorizes
another sunrise

the poem pulls
the drowning poet
from the current

and the ocean
breathes us all

MOWING

Not that I have a lawn
but I do mow now and then

I beat back the blackberry
and English ivy invaders

I remember the story
from the tractor driver

who accidentally mowed
over a spotted fawn

along with the tansy
and goldenrod

While I push my rotary
mower I've noticed

how the whirlwind
whips up the dead

leaves which seem
to leap like frogs

fleeing for their lives

SELF-IMPROVEMENT

I had been spending too much time
drying the bottoms of my feet
after a shower.

Every day my teeth would be sleepy
before noon. And my earlobes
had no ambition whatsoever.

From this rut, I could barely see.
I couldn't cough up a hairball
to save myself. I needed something

that could measure my worth
and make me feel valued
like an old coin with a rare mint mark.

So I started vacuuming my teeth
after flossing, and talking things over
with some dust bunnies peeking

from behind the kitchen stove. That got
me going. Now I can count
the change without taking it out

of my pocket. I can run to the mailbox
left handed. While I still can't answer
all of the questions inside my refrigerator,

I am ready for the path that leads
to the open door of the corridor
where I can relax and let go.

THE COMFORT CLASP

Clasp your hands in front of you,
all your fingers interlaced.

One thumb rests across the other thumb.
Which pinky is on the bottom?

Breathe deeply: once, twice.
Then rearrange the lacework,

placing the other pinky on the bottom
and the other thumb on top.

There seems to be a right way
and a wrong way for each of us.

This may be a social gesture,
signifying relaxation and calm.

It may be a prayer ritual remnant
or a lingering habit begun by accident.

TWO MEN

One man's fireworks
is another man's house fire.

What does your insurance
agent say about bottle rockets?

One man's garden
is another man's skin rash.

What does your dermatologist
say about lesions that weep?

One man's wife
is another man's mistress.

What does your attorney
say about community property?

One man's dream
is another man's nightmare.

What does your psychologist
say about therapy?

One man's vacation hike
is another man's death march.

What does your guide
say about hydration?

One man's slippery slope
is another man's grit.

DIFFICULT DAUGHTER

being a mom is ok
because frontward
or backward is alike

being a dad is ok too
because frontward
or backward is also alike

being a son is a little
more difficult because
there are so many nos

but try being a rethguad
that's even more difficult

POWER

a tornado sways
her hips
through Nebraska

a Right whale
takes a breath
before a nap

a childless couple
adopts a dog
from the pound

LAYOVER

Please watch your step
and hold onto the handrail
beep, beep, beep, beep, beep

Gilbert Mahoney, please meet
your party at the podium,
and hold onto the handrail

may I have your attention
please, carry on, beep, beep,
beep, beep, items are limited

and hold onto the handrail
please watch your step
and hold onto the handrail

to one bag and one personal,
beep, beep, beep, beep, item
such as a laptop or purse

medical items such as canes
are exempt from this restriction
please watch your beep, beep, beep

step and hold onto the handrail
Maureen Archer, meet your party
at the security checkpoint

on level three Candice Willows
please contact an operator
at the paging assistance location

and hold onto the handrail
Allen Chung please report
to the security checkpoint

A on level three, due to
beep, beep, beep, beep
and hold onto the handrail

increased security do not leave
baggage unattended all bags
are subject to search please

watch your step the walkway
is ending, hold onto beep, beep,
beep, beep, beep, the handrail

attention members of the military
the USO lounge is open
from 6:00 a.m. until 10:00 p.m.

and is located in Terminal A
across from the lost and found
please report any requests

to carry articles for others
to law enforcement or air
line authorities hold on

to the hand rail the walkway
is ending please contact
the paging assistance location

the walkway is ending
please watch your step
beep, beep, beep, beep

JACK

what I need
when I have
a flat tire

when apple juice
goes bad
applejack

without a jack cut
no cribbage player
can score perfectly

jack of spades
you're one-eyed
and well-groomed

jack of hearts
you too
are one-eyed

but sometimes you
separate the king
from the queen

blackjack you're exactly
twenty-one and ready
for a wild night

blackjack you've seen
some street fights
broken teeth and noses

Monterey jack
you're so mellow
you just melt

what the shift boss
says I don't know
jack of all trades

you know none

SMALL ANGELS

sparrows and hummingbirds
thrive in the bushes
that surround my house

at sunset the bats
come out to enjoy
the mosquitoes

the moth at my porch
light prays
I will come home

the tanagers tend
their nest in the hawthorn
near my garden

how many doves
have landed on my roof
without my even knowing?

small angels watch over me

FEATHERED STARS

sunset mentions eternity
to those still awake

doves and quail mix
on a gravel trail

feathered stars
of the hillside

the black bear walks
head first into a den

turns around
to face the night

lies down in the darkness
where all children begin

the river trundles stones
to the ocean

how many children
can you love?

sunrise mentions eternity
to those still asleep

COUGAR BREATH

Every breath
is the power
of the hillside

in my lungs
in camp
the flame

knows silence
knows whisper,
knows roar

the cougar purrs
fire walks
the mountainside

night coals
of Indian
paintbrush

leap the energy
of stars. Is this
sunrise or sunset?

Every breath
a taste
of the journey

every stride
the path
to eternity

Which ocean
is in front of me?

PEACEFUL SCREAMS

the beautiful
drooping bugle
of foxglove

calls reveille
to beavers
gnaw red alders

the molting crow
drops a feather
while azalea

perfumes the canyon
the fossilized moon
is a roving totem

born to know
every detail
of earth's shadow

overnight a chanterelle
pushes through
a century of duff

raindrops gather
to leap the falls
as a group

a bundle of gnawn
sticks rests
beside the fireplace

STUBBORN FAITH

salmon struggle
in low water

dry autumn
mushrooms

the hitchhiker stands
beside an empty road

a solo dove perches
above a dead partner

November robins
scout a frozen field

the match's flame
touches damp tinder

a campfire dents
the night sky

the cloudshine
of starlight

poets resubmit
rejected poems

PREDATOR

some of the deepest
questions come
from the ocean floor

some of the stunning
realizations float
right on the surface

almost any piece of wood
becomes an alligator
when it floats down a river

how deep does the shark
need to dive before it stops
casting a shadow?

LEFT HANDED?

The world is mostly made for righties
Chainsaws, scissors, and guitars

Lefties need patience,
Trial and error, innovation

A meaningful handshake
A right-handed compliment

Did you notice me this morning?
I was standing in line left handed!

It was a struggle but well worth
The time and practice

The proper way to mount
A Harley or horse is right leg over

Those blue, powdered nitrile gloves,
They transcend prejudice

So do drumsticks, spatulas, bicycle
Tires, raincoats, potato chips, and blankets

But bring in a left-handed sidearm pitcher
To face the left-handed slugger

Engaged, married, widowed?
Already one foot in the grave

Righty tighty, lefty loosey
Which one? No wrong turn

A SAILOR SPEAKS IN RETRONYMS

for Susan M. Livingstone

First she learns
the word or phrase
does not need to exist
until a new item expands
an idea by contrast.

Then she begins to say land line,
to distinguish it from cell phone.
Natural turf pops up because
Astro turf entered the stadium.
All guitars were acoustic

until the electric guitar
came on board. Still camera,
draft beer, manual transmission,
each had a turn at old becoming new.
Conventional warfare too

has many contrasts. Why was
the only woman to be Secretary
of Navy of the United States
the acting Secretary for
a total of fifteen days?

Male Sailors.

RITUAL MOSAIC

a little distance improves
the look of most mosaics

in a shallow pool starfish
know the tide is moving out

water ouzels do squats
on black basalt boulders

salmon return to the river
they recognize upstream

slow burning alder, madrone
and myrtle, bring out flavor

all trees know the strongest
branch begins at the heart

skinks do pushups
in the California sun

can the heart beat so hard
it breaks through the ribcage?

wolves and dogs bury bones

TOPOPHOBIA

If I arrive,
I will be there

and have nothing
to look forward to.

Looking backward
will be my power.

Yet my eyes have
no reverse,

so, always alive,
I must navigate

in the never-ending
moment of transport

because my arrival
is my journey end,

and I can not be
where I am not

yet ready to arrive,
my final resting

place.

LENTICEL

this is the birch box
a wood worker builds

from a hillside fallen tree
recovered from the river

the cuts and joinery
the carefully fitted lid

every time the carpenter
lifts the top out drifts

the yellow and orange
rustle of autumn leaves

a white throated sparrow
perches near a spring bud

the river never stops
quietly passing by

RIVER RÉSUMÉ

once I was a beam
of moonlight
touching the river

another time
a hoof track
on a sandbar

yet another time
a willow leaf
fallen into a rapids

want a free ride
to the ocean?
without prejudice

I provide lodging
for cutthroats
and suckers alike

with a small splash
I bring out the color
and pattern in granite

years at current
position?
a geologic epoch

though I can
be cool and quiet
on a summer day

I've drowned
more than a few
pairs of cousins

no one can step
into me
the same way twice

my thesis wears
down mountains
am I clear enough?

ACKNOWLEDGEMENTS

Some of the poems in this collection have appeared in the publications named below. The section titled "Lint" appeared in a chapbook from Finishing Line Press; the section titled "Forgotten Inventors" appeared in a pamphlet from Long House Press; the section titled "All This Tangling" appeared in a chapbook from Mardi Gras Press; the section titled "Shelter for Those Who Need It" (with the exception of "In China") appeared in a chapbook from 0_2 Press. "Snail" and "In the Hospital Paint Shop" both appeared in a chapbook titled *Wisconversation* from Elk Mound Press.

A.I.D. Review. Oklahoma City, OK. "Silent Language."
Alehouse. San Francisco, CA. "The Lost Part."
Alms House Press: Sampler. New York, NY. "Creating Sand."
And Review. Plain City, OH. "Almost Rain."
Argestes. South Amana, IA. "Lint."
Bloodroot. Thetford Center, VT. "Skunk Ethics."
Blue Light Review. Helena, MT. "The Horizon Is So Far."
Blue Pitcher. Greensboro, NC. "Detox."
Brother Jonathan Review. Arcata, CA. "A Brief History of Moisture."
Cadence of Hooves. Igo, CA. "Gypsy Freedom."
Caesura. San Jose, CA. "Potato," "Saltines," and "Peanuts."
Clifton. Cincinnati, OH. "Absorbing the Broadcast," "Where Boulders Split," and "Snowfall."
Cottonwood. Lawrence, KS. "The Way Time Passes."
Deviations. Ypsilanti, MI. "The Land" and "Aberdeen Harbour, Hong Kong."
Dos Passos Review. Farmville, VA. "Forgotten Inventors."
Earth's Daughters: Stormy Weather. Buffalo, NY. "Tsunami."
Eureka Reporter. Eureka, CA. "Liquid Fiber after the Funeral."
Fifth Wednesday. Lisle, IL. "Random Pattern."
Gambit. Parkersburg, WV. "The Cycle" and "The Marsh."
Greenfield Review. Greenfield Center, NY. "Incarceration."
Lake Effect. Erie, PA. "Surviving the House Fire," "Small Angels," and "Feathered Stars."
Moon City Review. Springfield, MO. "Jack."
Natural Bridge. St. Louis, MO. "Vibration."
North American Review. Cedar Falls, IA. "Mannequin with Teeth." (Pushcart nomination)
Northern Contours. Quincy, CA. "The Woman Who Walks the Beach at Dawn."
Pebbles. West Chester, PA. "Sanctuary" and "The Coastal Trail Turns Inland and Rises Up."
Permafrost. Fairbanks, AK. "Staying Close."

Plough: North Coast Review. Huron, OH. "Gloaming."

Poem. Huntsville, AL. "Two Men," "Predator," and "Lenticel."

Poem Sampling. Huntsville, AL. "Fewer Words" and "Snail."

Poetry in the Park. Columbus, OH. "Refreshment," "Camp Together," and "Raindrops."

Poetry Motel: The Inn, an Anthology. Duluth, MN. "Inspiration."

Poetry South. Itta Bena, MS. "The Comfort Clasp" and "River Résumé." (Pushcart nomination)

Portage. Stevens Point, WI. "Unglued" and "Liberation."

Rattle. Studio City, CA. 'The Power of Light."

Riverwind. Nelsonville, OH. "Stranger," "Around the Corner," and "Moving On."

Scent of Cedar. Santa Margarita, CA. "The Woman Who Walks the Beach at Dawn."

Snail Mail Review. Modesto, CA. "Self-Improvement" and "Pockets."

Soundings. Deerfield, IL. "The Horizon Is So Far," "Unglued," and "Snowfall."

Starnose. Huntsville, AL. "The Long Calm."

Steam Ticket. LaCrosse, WI. "On the Beach."

Toyon. Arcata, CA. "Chancing Dares" and "Truth."

Turtle Island Quarterly. Eureka, CA. "Cougar Breath" and "Even Breathing."

Valley Voices. Itta Bena, MS. "Layover" and "Mowing."

Witnessing Earth. Huntsville, AL. "The Coastal Trail Turns Inland and Rises Up."

Wordfire. Oroville, CA. "The Comfort Clasp."

World Order. Wilmette, IL. "Fewer Words."

ABOUT THE AUTHOR

Ken Letko teaches at the College of the Redwoods. He grew up on the seasonal rhythms of Lake Superior's Chequamegon Bay. Travel in the U.S., Canada, Mexico, Germany, Ecuador, and China globalized his awareness of the natural world and diverse cultures. For the last 25 years, he has lived in the magical intersection of ocean, redwoods, and mountains in Del Norte County on California's far Northern coast. He spent part of last summer as a fire lookout on Red Mountain in the Siskiyou Range. Ken's poems have appeared in five chapbooks and numerous small-press journals and anthologies. *Bright Darkness* is his first full-length book.